Christ's Priesthood

according to

The Epistle to the Hebrews

by

Rev. Ernest Lussier, S.S.S.

THE LITURGICAL PRESS
Collegeville
Minnesota

Imprimi potest: Rev. Normand Falardeau, S.S.S., Provincial.

Nihil obstat: William Heidt, O.S.B., *Censor deputatus.*
Imprimatur: ✠ George H. Speltz, Bishop of St. Cloud. St. Cloud, Minnesota, April 18, 1975.

ISBN 0-8146-0873-6

Preface

In our day when priests are going through a crisis of self-identity a return to the source of divine revelation, the holy Scriptures, should prove welcome and profitable.

The second Vatican Council states clearly: "The sacerdotal office of priests is conferred by that special sacrament through which priests, by the anointing of the Holy Spirit, are marked with a special character and are so configured to Christ the Priest that they can act in the person of Christ the Head. . . . Their ministry which takes its start from the gospel message, derives its power and force from the sacrifice of Christ" (Presbyterorum Ordinis #2). "Since they are ministers of God's Word, they should every day read and listen to that Word which they are required to teach to others. If they are at the same time preoccupied with welcoming this message into their own hearts, they will become ever more perfect disciples of the Lord" (#13).

By their Baptism and Confirmation all Christians also share in their own way in Christ's priesthood. "For their part, the faithful join in the offering of the Eucharist by virtue of their royal priesthood. They likewise exercise that priesthood by receiving the sacraments, by prayer and thanksgiving, by the witness of a holy life, and by self-denial and active charity" (Lumen Gentium #10).

—*Ernest Lussier, S.S.S.*

dedication

*To St. Peter Julien Eymard (1811–68)
The Priest of the Eucharist
Founder of the Congregation
of the Most Blessed Sacrament.
Canonized by Pope John XXIII
on Dec. 9, 1962*

Contents

1. Christ's Priestly Ministry (Heb. 2:5-18)

Christ is our priest, our leader on the way to salvation. His assuming a suffering human nature assured the efficacy and perfection of his ministry. Christ's Passion was not a defeat but a victory, according to God's saving plan. The sufferings of Jesus were neither arbitrary nor degrading, in view of what he was to God and men alike. — *page* 13

2. Christ's Priesthood and Ours (Heb. 4:14–5:10)

Among the biblical terms for priest (e.g., Levite, elder), mediator is perhaps the one which best denotes the nature of Christ's priesthood and ours. The conditions required by the priesthood are realized fully and eminently in Christ. Every priest is ordained to offer sacrifice to God as man's representative. He must be characterized by compassionate zeal and must be called by God. Christ is unlike other priests in that he shared the human condition in every way except that he had no sin. He became a perfect priest by learning to obey through suffering. His incarnation was his ordination; his life, culminating in his death and resurrection, is the exercise of his priesthood. — *page* 20

3. Christ's Priesthood According to the Order of Melchizedek (Heb. 7:1-10)

Melchizedek's priesthood, a royal priesthood, was superior to that of Aaron, yet it was only a figure of Christ's. Melchizedek blessed Abraham and accepted a tenth part of his booty. By name he was "king of justice"; as king of Salem, he was "king of peace." The absence of all records of his birth and death shows him as holding his priesthood by himself alone. More than Melchizedek, Christ is king of justice and peace; his priestly dignity is unique, his priesthood is eternal. Melchizedek was also superior to Abraham and Levi, and his priesthood was independent and universal and somehow eternal. All this is absolutely true of Christ alone.   — *page* 28

4. Christ's Eternal Priesthood (Heb. 7:11-28)

Christ's priesthood is heavenly in character, divine and everlasting in nature. It finds its exercise in his perpetual intercession on our behalf. The provisional character of the levitical priesthood gives way before the perpetuity of Christ's priesthood, a priesthood based on his own imperishable life, a power inherent in his nature and person as God's Son. Jesus is the only priest, and a priest forever. His perpetual intercession on our behalf is his supreme priestly function. Jesus is the ideal high priest, perfect in every respect in that office.   — *page* 35

5. Christ Our Mediator (Heb. 8:1-13)

The essential act of Christ's mediation is his worship of God, which is summarized and per-

petuated by his eternal priestly prayer and which
infinitely surpasses the ancient Mosaic sacrifices.
This is clear from the superiority of the sanctuary
in which Christ offers his sacrifice and from the
excellence of the new covenant which he established. Christ ministers in the heavenly
sanctuary, of which the earthly one was a mere
shadow. Christ is the only possible mediator between God and man, and his new covenant is
based on promises better than those of the old
covenant, inasmuch as it promises the writing of
an inward law upon man's heart, full and universal knowledge of God, and complete forgiveness of sin.   — *page* 44

6. The Excellence of Christ's Sacrifice (Heb. 9:1-12)

Christ's sacrifice is clearly superior to the
priestly service of the levitical ceremonial system, which was highlighted by the rite of atonement (Yom Kippur). The old sanctuary and the
rites of expiation were figurative in character.
Access to God is the final end and object of the
priesthood, and this is fully realized in Christ
alone. The scene, the offering, and the efficacy of
Christ's sacrifice show forth its superior excellence. Heaven is the temple which Jesus enters
by his glorious resurrection, and the blood of his
sacrifice is his own, which he offered once and
for all, winning for us an eternal redemption.
                                               — *page* 52

7. The Blood of Christ — A Perfect Sacrifice (Heb. 9:13-28)

With the Old Testament rites of expiation always in mind, the value and efficacy of Christ's

sacrifice is more clearly seen from the exceptional, purifying power of his Blood, through his eternal Spirit, his divine nature. Christ's expiation also inaugurates the new covenant. Finally, the blood of Christ is the perfect sacrifice which opens the perfect sanctuary of heaven and needs no repetition because of its absolute perfection. Christ's priestly intercession in the heavenly sanctuary, the supreme and essential exercise of his priestly ministry, is a description in ritual, liturgical language of his enthronement at the right hand of the Father. — *page* 59

8. The Perfect Efficacy of Christ's Sacrifice (Heb. 10:1-18)

Christ's sacrifice is superior not only to the general representative sacrifice of the Day of Atonement but to all the levitical sacrifices generally. It effects a perfect cure and needs no repetition; it also establishes a real community between the offerer and the victim and God himself, effected by perfect obedience to God's will. The efficacy of Christ's priestly work lies in the fact that his sacrifice is not only pleasing to God but has an absolute power, issuing from Christ's perfect sovereignty, the eternal perfection he has achieved in his glorification and enthronement at God's right hand. This is how he is able to sanctify us and make us, like him, perfect adorers of God. — *page* 65

CHRIST'S PRIESTHOOD

according to the

LETTER TO THE HEBREWS

1.

Christ's Priestly Ministry

HEBREWS 2:5-18

God did not make the world to come — that world of which we speak — subject to angels. [6] Somewhere this is testified to, in the passage that says:

"What is man that you should be mindful of him,
or the son of man that you should care for him?

[7] You made him for a little while lower than the angels;
you crowned him with glory and honor,

[8]   and put all things under his feet."

In subjecting all things to him, God left nothing un-subjected. At present we do not see all things thus subject, [9] but we do see Jesus crowned with glory and honor because he suffered death: Jesus, who was made for a little while lower than the angels, that through God's gracious will he might taste death for the sake of all men. [10] Indeed, it was fitting that when bringing many sons to glory God, for whom and through whom all things exist, should make their leader in the work of salvation perfect through suffering. [11] He who conse-crates and those who are consecrated have one and the same Father. Therefore he is not ashamed to call them brothers, [12] saying,

"I will announce your name to my brothers,
I will sing your praise in the midst of the assembly";

[13] and,

"I will put my trust in him";

and again,

"Here am I, and the children God has given me!"

[14] Now, since the children are men of blood and flesh,

Jesus likewise had a full share in ours, that by his death he might rob the devil, the prince of death, of his power, [15] and free those who through fear of death had been slaves their whole life long. [16] Surely he did not come to help angels, but rather the children of Abraham; [17] therefore he had to become like his brothers in every way, that he might be a merciful and faithful high priest before God on their behalf, to expiate the sins of the people. [18] Since he was himself tested through what he suffered, he is able to help those who are tempted.

The Epistle to the Hebrews demonstrates the excellence and holiness of the Christian religion over Judaism from the superiority of its mediator, Jesus Christ, considering his person (1:4–4:13), his priesthood (4:14–7:28), and his sacrifice (8:1–10:18).

Personally, Jesus, as God's Son, is superior to all the mediators of the Old Testament, especially the angels (1:4–2:18) and Moses (3:1–4:13). According to Jewish belief, the law was ministered by angels (2:2), but even the dignity of these, the highest representatives of the dispensation, is as far below that of Christ as the title of minister is below that of the incommunicable name of divine Majesty (1:4).

Christ is the Son of God; the angels are his servants (1:14). He is the creator and master of all things; the angels are busy ministering to men (1:5-14). And if the law given by the angels commanded obedience, how much more the revelation made by Jesus Christ (2:1-4)!

Christ humbled himself below the angels to be like us men, whom he wanted to save. According to God's plan, Christ's assumption of a human nature was indispensable for his mission of salvation, yet in no way derogated from his essential dignity. Christ's abasement was necessary to assure the efficacy and perfection of his priesthood. He thus became a perfect priest capable of leading us to glory (2:5-18).

Glory came through humiliation, and priesthood through death. It was necessary that Jesus, author of man's salvation, be made like to those whom he saves, and in their likeness suffer and die. It is thus that he became the merciful and faithful high priest of mankind.

Christ is our perfect mediator and priest because he is God's Son and our Savior — such is briefly the teaching of the first two chapters of the Epistle to the Hebrews. Being at the same time God and man, Christ is essentially priest, with full power to mediate between God and man. He joins in his person, in an unrivaled unity, all possible powers and avenues of mediation, ascending to God and descending to men.

Christ is the head of the messianic kingdom (2:5-18). He is, as it were, the leader who at the last moment takes over an army in full rout and saves it from complete disaster by utterly destroying Satan's empire. God gave to him, not to the angels, the promise of empire over "the world to come" (2:5-9). By humbling himself below the angels in his incarnation and in his death, he obtained the realization of the divine promises, namely, triumph for himself and salvation for men (2:10-18).

This is the answer to the Jewish objection that Jesus, far from appearing as one superior to the angels, was seen as man, in such conspicuous humiliation that he suffered a felon's death instead of mounting a worldly throne.

The "world to come" (2:5) is the messianic age, the Christian dispensation in its double phase — temporal and eternal. It is the kingdom of God begun on earth in its militant stage and blossoming into glory at the end of time. It is the new order of things, moral and spiritual, the salvation (1:14; 2:2-3) brought by Christ, but always pressing forward to fuller manifestations and receiving consummation at his glorious coming (9:28).

Christians already taste the good things to come (6:5), and are even now associated with the elect (12:23) because of Christ, who bridges time and eternity for them.

Psalm 8 (Heb. 2:6-8) is a panegyric of man, like Hamlet's ("What a piece of work is man! How noble in reason! How infinite in faculties! In form and moving, how express and admirable! In action how like an angel!"), but with a religious note of wonder and gratitude to God. In its literal sense the psalm sings the glorious place of man in creation. Feeble and mortal by nature (2:6), he has received from God a noble estate, a nature which is closely related to pure spirit, a crown of honor and glory which makes him king of creation, with universal dominion over all the works of God's hands (2:7-8).

Christ being the representative *par excellence* of humanity, it is in him that the absolute and universal messianic empire will be realized. Using the words of the Psalmist more than his thought, our author (2:8) interprets "all things" as including the kingdom of "the world to come" (2:5). But Christ's supremacy, at the present time, is clearly not completely effective (2:8).

We find expressed here the anguish and disappointment of the first Christians, who, despised and persecuted, awaited the coming of the reign of God on earth (2 Peter 3:4). All should know, however, that

Christ has already entered into glory, even if his militant kingdom is still in progress.

Everything is subject to him even now by right and in hope. His reign, however, is not undisputed, but he will annihilate all his enemies (1:13), and his kingdom will ultimately obtain its full and triumphant consummation (1 Cor. 15:25-28).

> The work is not complete
> One world I know, and see
> It is not at his feet—
> Not! Not! Is this the sum?
> —T. E. Brown

No, it is not the sum. We do see Jesus enthroned, with the full prospect of ultimate triumph (2:9). All the just will then obey him freely forever, and the unjust will be forced to submit to his rule.

To the eyes of faith, Christ's Passion is not a defeat but a victory. He experienced the full bitterness of death, but his abasement was momentary and merited for him the glory of heaven. Christ is glorified because he suffered, and his triumph consecrates the redemptive value of his death in favor of all mankind.

Christ's glory is the prelude of ours. His glorification is the guarantee that all men, his brothers, will ultimately share his bliss, thus experiencing God's gracious kindness in fulfilling his original counsel of love, in spite of man's sin. The crowning of Christ with heavenly glory is a sign that the redemption of man has been successful. His reign in heaven is sacerdotal. He is there to prepare a place for us (John 14:3), and he is constantly interceding in our behalf (Heb. 7:25).

The earthly experiences of Jesus do not diminish his glory but rather minister to it. The Passion, in

God's plan, was most fitting (2:10). Christ had to re-
semble us (2:11-13), and this solidarity has proved
most fruitful (2:14-18).

Only by suffering could Christ save his brother
men who lay under the tyranny of death (2:15). To
die for everyone meant that Jesus had to enter human
life and identify himself with men (2:11-14). Now suffering is the badge and lot of the race, and a Savior
must be a sufferer if he is to carry out God's saving
purpose (2:10). The sufferings of Jesus were neither
arbitrary nor degrading, but normal and natural, in
view of what he was to God and men alike.

Hebrews 2:10 is a short treatise on the fittingness of
Christ's Passion, which is considered in relation to
God, to men, and to Christ.

God did not have to save us, and once he decided to
do so, there were many different ways to accomplish
his purpose. He chose a means in harmony with his
nature and perfections, worthy alike of his character
and his wisdom.

For us men, Christ's Passion became the basis of
our vocation as God's children and of our ultimate
glorification. The heavenly Father wanted sons to
share his celestial glory, and as many as possible. To
this end, Christ's Passion was a most apt means.

Finally, salvation by suffering was most becoming
to Christ's role as the author of our redemption.
Christ, in fact, is the captain, the pioneer, of our salvation, its originator and personal source, our guide
and exemplar who goes before and points the way to
his followers (12:2). Sufferings constitute both his
training in leadership and the means of redemption
in which his leadership attains its end.

Jesus is made perfect through suffering, which
leads him to the highest degree of excellence in every
respect: moral perfection, since he practices every vir-

tue; perfection as mediator, acting as our brother and gaining our confidence, and at the same time offering to God the most acceptable sacrifice; finally, perfection of merit, giving him the right to the highest glory and to universal sovereignty. The perfection of the priest of the new covenant includes being a victim, and so it is by the sufferings of the Passion that Jesus could accomplish perfectly his office of priestly salvation.

2.

Christ's Priesthood and Ours

HEBREWS 4:14–5:10

Since, then, we have a great high priest who has passed through the heavens, Jesus, the Son of God, let us hold fast to our profession of faith. We do not have a high priest who is unable to sympathize with our weakness, but one who was tempted in every way that we are, yet never sinned. 16 So let us confidently approach the throne of grace to receive mercy and favor and to find help in time of need.

1 Every high priest is taken from among men and made their representative before God, to offer gifts and sacrifices for sins. 2 He is able to deal patiently with erring sinners, for he himself is beset by weakness 3 and so must make sin offerings for himself as well as for the people. 4 One does not take this honor on his own initiative, but only when called by God as Aaron was. 5 Even Christ did not glorify himself with the office of high priest; he received it from the One who said to him,

"You are my son;
today I have begotten you";
6 just as he says in another place,
"You are a priest forever,
according to the order of Melchizedek."

7 In the days when he was in the flesh, he offered prayers and supplications with loud cries and tears to God, who was able to save him from death, and he was heard because of his reverence. 8 Son though he was, he learned obedience from what he suffered; 9 and when perfected, he became the source of eternal salvation for all who obey him, 10 designated by God as high priest according to the order of Melchizedek.

The ordinary word for *priest* in the Old Testament is *kohen*, a term that is still preserved as the common Jewish family name Cohen. Unfortunately the original semantic derivation of the form is unknown, although the duties of the Old Testament priests in the worship of God and in the ministry of his word are quite clear.

The name *Levite* was also originally applied to the Old Testament priests. The term refers to the particular clan of Levi which was chosen by God to exercise the special functions of his worship (Num. 3:12; Deut. 10:8). At a later period, however, the name Levite indicated one who belonged to a rank of cultic servants lower than the priests and who was charged with the menial services in the temple (1 Chron. 23).

The Greek word for *priest* is *hiereus*, meaning "sacrificer." As a rule, the New Testament writers did not use this qualifier for Christ, no doubt because the word referred to a well-defined function with which Christ's priesthood had practically nothing in common. In the Epistle to the Hebrews, however, the writer's special outlook frequently prompts him to apply the term to Christ (Heb. 5:6; 7:15).

The first Christian priests are called "overseers" (1 Tim. 3:2) and "elders" (Titus 1:5). Our English word *priest* is derived from the Greek term for "elder." The New Testament priests are also described as pastors or shepherds (Eph. 4:11-12), as leaders who preside over the Christian community (1 Thess. 5:12) and command with authority (Acts 15:22), as subordinate assistants of Christ and stewards of the mysteries of God (1 Cor. 4:1), and as ministers of the New Covenant (2 Cor. 3:6).

' The term *mediator*, however (Heb. 8:6; 9:15; 12:24), is perhaps the one that characterizes best of all the nature of Christ's priesthood and ours. This idea of Christ's priestly work of mediation is a favorite theme in the Epistle to the Hebrews.

The addressees of this epistle were troubled by many serious vexations (10:32-34) and were apparently attracted by the Jewish worship which, thanks to the good will of Agrippa II, was being conducted with renewed splendor in the temple at Jerusalem. The author consequently intends to prove the strict superiority of the new law over the old. He does so by considering the person and dignity of Christ (1:1–4:13), and by establishing a long parallel between Christ's priesthood (4:14–7:28) and his sacrifice (8:1–10:18) as compared to the levitical priesthood and sacrifices.

The epistle abounds with wonderful insights into the mystery of Christ's priesthood. One passage is especially illuminating; it is the Pauline *definition of Christ's priesthood* (4:14–5:10), which serves as an introduction to the establishment of the superiority of Christ's priesthood over that of the Old Testament. After a short prelude (4:14-16), the writer indicates the conditions required of any priest (5:1-4) and shows how they were realized in Christ (5:5-10).

Christ's dignity is infinite, since he is the very Son of God (1:1–4:13); at the same time, however, he is very close to us, having become one of us. Our confidence in him, our high priest — in fact, our only mediator (1 Tim. 2:5) — should be unbounded (Heb. 4:14-16). He has already entered into God's immediate presence and will introduce us in due time (4:14). He is able to sympathize with our weaknesses because he has shared our human condition and, like us, has been tested in every way, but never sinned (4:15). He is thus able to bring us closer to God, with whom he dwells, that we may receive mercy and in God's grace find timely help (4:16).

We find in Hebrews 5:1 an excellent *general view* of what every priest must be. In relation to his origin: he is taken from among men, since he must act for men and consequently be acceptable to them. In relation to his role or character, his distinctive nature or quality: he is appointed men's representative or agent before God. He is not a priest for himself; it is in the name of men and in their behalf that he presents himself before God. And finally, in relation to his function: the priest offers sacrifice. Since man is a fallen creature, the gifts offered to God naturally assume the character of sacrifices for sin.

After this summary view of the priesthood, the author insists on the priest's *human qualities* (5:2-3). They are summarized in compassionate zeal and leniency in moral judgment. The priest must know how to moderate his feelings and deal gently with people, avoiding undue severity. Most people are ignorant and erring (5:2) through passion and weakness, and really not maliciously defiant in their offenses. Leniency is all the more required since the priest himself is the victim of moral infirmity and must offer reparation for himself as well as for the people (5:3).

The priest must be a man of sympathy born of experience. He is not by definition a paragon of moral integrity, or an austere saint in whom the passions of humanity have been quenched, but one who, like his people, is beset by infirmity and owes the debt of moral weakness.

Like Peter, the priest must first convert himself and then lend some of his strength to his brethren (Luke 22:32). Notice how Peter's famous question about the limits of forgiveness was put before his own fall (Matthew 18:21); our Lord answered that forgiveness is beyond calculating (18:22). The humiliation of a moral fall is salutary and sobering, wearing off some of the edges of our pride and high-handed severity. On the other hand, it cannot be the occasion for laxity and negligence.

The parable of the unmerciful servant (Matthew 18:23-35) is also well quoted here.

In this respect Christ is unlike other priests, although he did know and feel the terrible strain of temptation (in the wilderness, in Gethsemani, on the Cross) and surely always showed himself kind, compassionate, and zealous for the expiation of the sins of his brethren.

Finally, the priest, being mediator between God and men, must be agreeable to both parties. We have seen his relation to men (Heb. 5:1-3); it remains to state his relation to God (5:4).

The priest has a distinctive office, yet his priesthood is not precisely the prize of successful effort. He is a priest mainly because God calls him. The necessity of a divine call (5:4) is established by the story of Aaron and his sons (Num. 16–17) and the rejection of the clans of Core, Datham, and Abiram. It follows also from the very nature of the priesthood and of the priestly requisites described.

In fact, how could a man, a sinner like the rest, dare approach God, especially in the name of mankind, unless God called him and entrusted him with this mission? Such a responsible office cannot be filled by self-election. No man who would think so highly of himself as to deem himself worthy of such an honor would be likely to show compassion for others, which must spring from true self-knowledge.

Christ realizes fully and eminently all these priestly requirements (5:5-10). The application follows an inverted order: first his divine vocation (5:5-6, corresponding to 5:4); then (corresponding to 5:1-3) his power of sympathy with humankind (5:7-8) and the exercise of his priestly office (5:9-10).

Becoming man without ceasing to be God (5:5), Christ became by that very fact the only true mediator between God and the human race, and consequently the sovereign Pontiff *par excellence*. Theologians have always rightly pointed to the Incarnation as Christ's sacerdotal investiture or consecration. The second text (5:6) shows how Christ can be true priest without descending from Aaron, an important problem for the first educated Jewish converts.

Jesus endured suffering (5:7-8) and thus became the perfect priest (5:9-10). In the clearness and emphasis with which they portray the completeness of our Lord's humanity, verses 7-8 are unique in the epistles.

Through suffering, Christ learned how to obey (5:7). He did not take the priesthood to himself; he showed a perfect obedience to the Father. Far from seeking the priesthood, he shrank in agony from it and accepted it only in filial submission to the will of God. Son though he was, he was not exempted from terrible suffering. He shared the universal human experience of suffering, grief, and death.

Christ prayed all through his earthly life (5:7), but especially at his agony (Matthew 26:36-44) and death (Matthew 27:50). Note the characteristics of that prayer — it is humble, instant, persevering, ardent, submissive. Its object manifests great compassion and contains deep encouragement for our weak flesh (Matthew 26:41). Jesus knew that his Father could save him from death and expressed his natural apprehension and the desires of his sensible nature, which in spontaneous horror shrank from death; yet he prayed that his Father's will should be done

(Matthew 26:39, 42). He prayed to obtain the strength to perform, in spite of the extreme repugnance of his human sensibility, the sacrifice required by God.

Hence the efficacy of his prayer. There was in the agony of his prayer a depth of religion and filial reverence that could not but be heard (Heb. 5:7). And so in the weakness of his humanity, our model of obedience (5:8) — an obedience that he carried to the utmost limit of death (Phil. 2:8) — our only possible Savior, Jesus Christ, becomes the perfect priest, our chief and leader, our high priest.

Made perfect by suffering, Jesus became to all men, who by obeying him share in his obedience, the author of a salvation that is eternal (Heb. 5:9). He thus exercises his priestly office and is hailed by God in the eternal sphere, eternal high priest (5:10).

The *perfection* of Christ, as priest and victim, is affirmed categorically (5:9) and embraces the vast horizon of the context. It is moral perfection, achieved by the heroism of his obedience. It is perfection of salvation, obtaining all the graces which assure forever the holiness and happiness of the elect. It is also exemplary perfection by which he shows himself as the model to be imitated and the leader to be followed. In a word, it is *priestly* perfection, which gains our confidence in our knowledge that he understands us and which makes him pray to his Father for us, the way he prayed for himself and was heard. Finally and consequently, it is a perfection of glory, raising him and us to the heights of heaven. Christ's perfection and that of his priests is, then, personal perfection with the power of granting eternal salvation.

The Incarnation is Christ's ordination to the priesthood; his sacrifice on the Cross and its ratification by the heavenly Father are its ultimate consummation and the dawn of his eternal priesthood.

In a last moment of recollection, we recall with Saint Paul (Tim. 2:5) that just as there is but one God, there is also but one mediator between God and men — Christ Jesus. We who are priests thank God for the grace of our priesthood and deplore our many negligences in the performance of our sacred ministry.

3.

Christ's Priesthood according to the Order of Melchizedek

HEBREWS 7:1-10

This Melchizedek, king of Salem and priest of the Most High God, met Abraham returning from his defeat of the kings and blessed him. ² And Abraham apportioned to him one tenth of all his booty. His name means "king of justice"; he was also king of Salem, that is, "king of peace." ³ Without father, mother or ancestry, without beginning of days or end of life, like the Son of God he remains a priest forever.
⁴ See the greatness of this man to whom Abraham the patriarch gave one tenth of his booty! ⁵ The law provides that the priests of the tribe of Levi should receive tithes from the people, their brother Israelites, even though all of them are descendants of Abraham; ⁶ but Melchizedek, who was not of their ancestry, received tithes of Abraham and blessed him who had received God's promises. ⁷ It is indisputable that a lesser person is blessed by a greater. ⁸ And whereas men subject to death receive tithes, Scripture testifies that this man lives on. ⁹ Levi, who receives tithes, was, so to speak, tithed in the person of his father, ¹⁰ for he was still in his father's loins when Melchizedek met Abraham.

This passage establishes the excellence of our Lord's priesthood by comparing it with that of Melchizedek. Melchizedek's priesthood was much superior to that of Aaron and of his priests, yet it was only a figure and shadow of Christ's priesthood.

Melchizedek is presented not merely as a type of Christ but almost as an archetype or prototype, as a mysterious personage who is somehow identified with the one he prefigures. It follows that much of what is said here about Melchizedek (especially in verses 3 and 8) is out of focus if applied to him, and really refers only to Jesus, our high priest.

The priesthood of Melchizedek is recognized in Genesis 14:17-20; in Psalm 109:4, the priesthood of the Messiah is identified with that of Melchizedek. It is a royal priesthood. The Messiah, like Melchizedek, will be king and priest, and that forever.

Our passage (Heb. 7:1-10) is best interpreted as a midrash on Genesis 14:17-20. This characteristic, more or less free, Jewish elaboration of the Melchizedek story probably served an apologetical purpose in the sacred writer's mind. His readers needed to be shown how a Jew could be justified in so embracing Christianity as to break with the Jewish system of worship and to surrender the Jewish system of sacrifices.

The mysterious figure Melchizedek is introduced (Heb. 7:1-3), and his priesthood is shown to be superior to the levitical priesthood (7:4-10).

First the characteristics of Melchizedek (7:1-3). The sacred writer mentions some positive facts related to Melchizedek: the description of his person, his meeting with Abraham, and Abraham's offering (7:1-2a). He then indicates the significance of his character from the interpretation of his titles as "king of justice" and "king of peace," and also from the portraiture which can be deducted from the silence of Scripture (7:2b-3).

The demonstration begins with the historical facts

relative to Melchizedek (7:1-2a). According to
Genesis 14:17-20, Melchizedek, king of Salem, went
out to meet Abraham as the patriarch was returning
from the rout of Chodorlahomor and his allies. Melchizedek bestowed his blessing on Abraham and accepted a tenth part of the booty that had been taken.

"Salem" is an archaic name for Jerusalem, the city
where Yahweh would later choose to dwell. Melchizedek was king there and a priest of the true God,
the most high God of heaven and all creation, even
before the institution of the levitical priesthood. Melchizedek appears again in Psalm 109:4 as a figure of
the Messiah, king and priest.

Later patristic allegorism has seen in the bread and
wine brought to Abraham (Gen. 14:18) a figure of the
Eucharist and even a true sacrifice forecasting the
Eucharistic sacrifice. This interpretation has found
place in the Canon of the Mass. It is quite possible
that the mention of bread and wine in Genesis 14:18
supposes the offering of a sacrifice, but the point is
not taken up in the Epistle to the Hebrews. The inci-
dent was apparently irrelevant to the author's particular purpose in writing and beyond his doctrinal
perspective and theological outlook.

The historical details relative to Melchizedek having been noted, the writer of the epistle goes on to
interpret the scriptural narrative insofar as it affects
the view of Melchizedek's character and person absolutely (7:2b-3). He also points out its bearing on his
position in relation to Abraham and the levitical
priests (7:4-10). Melchizedek's typical character is
shown to be indicated positively by what is said of
him (7:2b), and negatively by what is not said (7:3).

Thus, three distinct features are noted in which
Melchizedek points to Christ: his name and title, "king
of justice" and "king of peace"; his detachment from

all priestly descent, holding his priesthood himself alone; the absence of all records of his birth and death.

In other words, the record of Melchizedek points to Christ's character, his office, and his person or nature. More perfectly than Melchizedek, Christ is king of justice and peace; his priestly dignity is unique, and his priesthood strictly eternal.

Melchizedek's name and the name of his city are taken to correspond with the actual traits of the character of the Messiah — a priest whose reign will be *par excellence* a reign of justice and peace. Justice and peace, in fact, are essential features of the messianic rule (Ps. 71; Is. 9:5; Eph. 2:14), the two great fruits of salvation, and a summary of the notion and office of the priesthood.

The delineation of Melchizedek is further expressed by what is not said about him. The silence of Scripture is treated as having a hidden meaning. Melchizedek stands unique and isolated both in his person and in his history. He is not connected with any known line, and his life has no recorded beginning or close (Heb. 7:3).

Genealogy was essential for the levitical priests, who had to be descendants of Aaron (Num. 16–17) and born of a Jewish mother (Ezek. 44:22; Ezra 2:61-62). Christ, like Melchizedek, had no need of a genealogy to be priest. His priesthood does not depend on his ancestors but on a personal title completely independent of his earthly father and mother. It is inherent in himself as God's only Son (Heb. 7:28) and absolutely independent of hereditary transmission.

Finally, Christ's priesthood is not only unique and exclusive but also permanent, even eternal. Scripture records nothing about Melchizedek's birth or death, although there is nothing in the texts to indicate a miraculous translation or the like. This negative eternity, or apparent independence in relation to time and duration, is explained as foreshadowing the positive eternity of Christ's priesthood (7:3).

Our Lord's eternal pre-existence was implied in Hebrews 1:3, but the stress here is on his endless life. Note also that, for Christ, this permanence in the priesthood is based not merely on the eternity of his divine nature (1:11-12), but also, and perhaps more explicitly, on the permanence of his resurrected life (7:16, 23-28).

Having discussed the historical notice of Melchizedek in itself, the writer goes on to consider his priesthood in relation to that of the law, and demonstrates the superiority of Melchizedek over Abraham and Levi (7:4-10). Melchizedek received the tithes of the choicest spoils from Abraham (7:4-6a) and blessed him (7:6b-7). And the levitical priests exercised their functions as mere men subject to death (7:8) and implicitly paid tithes to Melchizedek by the hands of Abraham, their father (7:9-10).

The tithes paid to the levitical priest (Deut. 14:22) were both the salary for the priestly office and homage to the eminent dignity of the priesthood. If then Levi himself, in Abraham, paid tithes to Melchizedek, it follows that Melchizedek's priesthood was of a superior type.

The levitical priest had to be able to list his genealogy with great exactness as a qualification for his office (Neh. 7:64). Now even Abraham, the father of the Jewish people, pays tithes to Melchizedek, a stranger whose greatness does not depend on his genealogy or tribe, on law or convention, but only on an inherent personal title, his personal authority and dignity. Thus in Melchizedek we have a distinct and independent priesthood, a univeral priesthood not limited to one people or one race.

Another sign of the personal dignity of Melchizedek is the blessing that he imparted to the patriarch Abraham, to whom had been given the divine promises of blessings for all mankind (Gen. 12:2-3). The one who blessed with authority and in virtue of his functions is clearly superior to the one who is blessed (Heb. 7:6-7).

Actually, through Jesus Christ the blessing of Abraham was extended to all the nations (Gal. 3:14). And the attitude in which Jesus was last seen by the Apostles at his Ascension (Luke 24:51) signified that his work in heaven would be to pour out blessings on the faithful, eliciting ever-renewed benedictions from men to God (Eph. 1:3).

Melchizedek was superior to Abraham; he was superior also to the levitical priesthood (Heb. 7:8-10). This is shown both by the nature of the priests themselves (7:8) and by the position that Levi, the common ancestor, occupied toward Abraham (7:9-10).

The levitical priests were mortal men, while Melchizedek is presented as living on indefinitely (7:8). A naturally transient priesthood gives way to one that is eternal. Here again, as in 7:3, Jesus alone is really in focus — he who, once raised from the dead, will never die again (Rom. 6:9); he who is priest forever, always living to plead our cause (Heb. 7:25).

A possible objection is answered in 7:9-10: Abraham was not a priest, and the levitical priesthood with its prerogatives had not yet been instituted in his time. The solution of the difficulty is that Abraham included in himself, as the depositary of the divine promise and the divine blessing, all the forms, as yet undifferentiated, in which they were to be embodied.

The descendants of Abraham cannot but occupy a lower position in the presence of one who appears as Abraham's superior. Abraham's descendants were included in him, not only because he was their physical forefather but also because he was the recipient of the divine promises, in which the fullness of the race in its manifold developments were included. And Levi includes his descendants in his own person, just as he was himself included in Abraham. The same, of course, could be said of Christ, who was a descendant of Abraham, as Levi was, but the question is non-existent for our author, who views Melchizedek as practically identified with Christ.

We admire and adore Christ's priesthood according to the order of Melchizedek. It is a royal priesthood, a universal priesthood, the priesthood of the new and better covenant (7:22), of the "better hope" (7:19); an eternal priesthood, the priesthood of God's own Son (7:28) and of our risen Lord.

Jerusalem, the holy city, also appears to us as a wonderful object of contemplation. It is the focal point of both testaments: the capital of David, the witness of our Lord's death and resurrection, the prefiguration of the Church and of heaven, our eternal dwelling place.

Priests share in Christ's priesthood; our Lord acts on earth through their ministry. They are his ministers (Rom. 15:16), his envoys, his ambassadors (2 Cor. 5:20). Like him, they are priests forever after the manner of Melchizedek by reason of their sacerdotal character, which guarantees not only the power of their orders but also the graces necessary for their exalted state of life.

4.
Christ's Eternal Priesthood

HEBREWS 7:11-28

If, then, perfection had been achieved through the levitical priesthood (on the basis of which the people received the law), what need would there have been to appoint a priest according to the order of Melchizedek, instead of choosing a priest according to the order of Aaron? [12] When there is a change of priesthood, there is necessarily a change of law. [13] Now he of whom these things are said was of a different tribe, none of whose members ever officiated at the altar. [14] It is clear that our Lord rose from the tribe of Judah, regarding which Moses said nothing about priests. [15] The matter is clearer still if another priest is appointed according to the likeness of Melchizedek: [16] one who has become a priest, not in virtue of a law expressed in a commandment concerning physical descent, but in virtue of the power of a life which cannot be destroyed. [17] Scripture testifies: "You are a priest forever according to the order of Melchizedek."

[18] The former commandment has been annulled because of its weakness and uselessness, [19] for the law brought nothing to perfection. But a better hope has supervened, and through it we draw near to God. [20] This has been confirmed by an oath. The priests of the old covenant became priests without an oath, [21] unlike Jesus to whom God said:

"The Lord has sworn, and he will not
    repent:
  'You are a priest forever, according
    to the order of Melchizedek.' "

[22] Thus has Jesus become the guarantee of a better covenant. [23] Under the old covenant there were many priests

35

because they were prevented by death from remaining in office; ²⁴ but Jesus, because he remains forever, has a priesthood which does not pass away. ²⁵ Therefore he is always able to save those who approach God through him, since he forever lives to make intercession for them.

²⁶ It was fitting that we should have such a high priest: holy, innocent, undefiled, separated from sinners, higher than the heavens. ²⁷ Unlike the other high priests, he has no need to offer sacrifice day after day, first for his own sins and then for those of the people; he did that once for all when he offered himself. ²⁸ For the law sets up as high priests men who are weak, but the word of the oath which came after the law appoints as priest the Son, made perfect forever.

The Epistle to the Hebrews fixes our attention mainly on the heavenly character of Christ's priesthood, its divine and everlasting nature, and the perpetual intercession (7:25) in which it finds its exercise. By this priestly prayer Christ is perpetually our Savior, applying to us the fruits of his redemptive sacrifice.

In the first section of the epistle (4:14–7:28), the author shows the superiority of the priesthood of Jesus Christ over the levitical priesthood. The excellence of our Lord's priesthood is demonstrated by comparing it with that of Melchizedek (7:1-28). The mysterious Melchizedek is introduced (7:1-3), and his priesthood is shown to be superior to the levitical priesthood (7:4-10). Finally, Christ, priest according to the order of Melchizedek, is shown to surpass in dignity all the priests of the old law (7:11-28).

The provisional and temporary character of the levitical priesthood (7:11-19) gives way before the perpetuity of the new priesthood founded on a divine oath (7:20-25). Hence the absolute perfection of Christ's priesthood (7:26-28). The superiority of Christ's priesthood is proved (7:11-19) by strict reasoning based on the fact that the levitical priesthood was replaced by God (7:11). It would clearly be contrary to the divine wisdom to replace a religious economy by another if this substitution did not mark some progress.

The transitory and imperfect character of the levitical priesthood implies also the abrogation of the old law (7:12). The priesthood, in fact, was the vital center of the whole ancient system of law and the first cause of its effectiveness. The levitical priests were the representatives of the law, they drew their authority from the law, and they themselves maintained and guarded the law. A defective priesthood would then necessarily vitiate the whole economy, for the law depended on the priesthood.

The appearance of another priest of a different and superior order (7:4-10) supersedes the whole previous system, since the levitical priesthood was the core and essence of the whole law (7:12). And there is a new priesthood, the one of which the Psalmist spoke.

In Jesus, who was not of the family of Aaron (7:11, 13) but of Judah (7:14) is verified the prediction of Psalm 110:4 (7:17). He is a priest according to the likeness of Melchizedek (7:15), for his priesthood is not flesh-bound like the levitical one, but fully supernatural because it is based on an imperishable life (7:16). It is all the difference between the temporary and the eternal, the earthly and the heavenly. The Old Testament priest was appointed by law, a regulation external to himself. Jesus is priest by a power inherent to his own nature and person.

The Aaronic priests succeeded one another by virtue of heredity. Their priesthood was essentially connected with their fleshly nature, so none of them could enjoy the sacerdotal dignity in perpetuity. With Christ it is otherwise. He is a priest forever. His priesthood is spiritual, far above the accidents of time and space. On him death has no hold. His life was really not diminished or destroyed by his cruel death on the Cross but expanded, enlarged, magnified. His death was the voluntary sacrifice which reunited him to his Father, as is witnessed by his glorious Ascension and his blessed existence at the right of his Father.

Christ, our high priest, exercises his functions by virtue of an indestructible life (7:16), which is his, not merely because of his glorious resurrection, but especially because of his exaltation (7:26) as God's Son (7:28), and so is eternal, since it had no beginning and will have no end. His eternal livingness is at once the source and the measure of his priestly qualifications; and the measure being thus immeasurable, it sets forth the immeasurable superiority of his priesthood over Aaron's priesthood.

Christ's priestly office is neither inherited nor transmitted. He is a priest in virtue of what he is; and since his being transcends time, he is a priest forever. Hereditary succession has no possible comparison with the inherent personality of the Son.

In Christ the imperfect makes way for the perfect (7:18-19). The abrogation of the Old Testament priesthood entailed the abrogation of the Mosaic law. The law could not lead to true holiness. The gospel, on the contrary, introduces us to a better hope, which draws us near to God by the graces it confers.

The complete destruction of sin was not possible by the law because of its basic imperfection (7:18). The new order by which it is replaced is permanent and effective, being bound up with the higher and nobler hope of the gospel, which enables men to "draw near to God" (7:19) not merely in symbol but in spiritual reality. In Christ, Christian hope thus fulfills completely the idea and function of the priesthood, which is to draw men into fellowship with God, a communion which is the very essence of religion. And though it be only a hope and not yet a perfect realization, it is of such a nature that it already enters within the veil of eternity and binds us fast to the world to come.

The new priesthood, based on a solemn divine promise or oath, is of necessity eternal, all the more so since that oath contained a promise of eternal endurance (7:20-25). An oath is not given lightly, especially when it comes from God (7:21), and it is all the more important, since the levitical priesthood was not established with such a solemn sanction (7:20). Jesus, our priest, has thus become the surety for a much superior covenant (7:22).

Scripture describes at great length (Exod. 28; Lev. 8–9) the consecration of Aaron and his sons as high priests. For Jesus, the consecrator is God instead of Moses; the assistants are the angels; the theater is at once heaven, which the Son of God does not leave, and also the earth, to which he descends by the Incarnation. For unction, instead of the blood of animal sacrifices and the perfumed oil which scented Aaron's vestments, the divinity itself invested the whole humanity of Jesus and enriched it with the plenitude of graces, which would overflow to all the members of his Mystical Body.

As through the Son of Man the covenant becomes established, so in him it remains secure; the words addressed by God to him as priest and king contain the pledge of its validity and permanence. Jesus is

thus the mediator, the surety or pledge of a much
superior covenant, the guarantor on God's behalf for
us, but also on our behalf for God. This surety consists in his guaranteeing the fulfillment of God's
promises to men, but also in making satisfaction to
God for the sins of men. The twofold guarantee made
him a perfect mediator: one who could provide that a
covenant of assured blessing for mankind would not
be inconsistent with the holiness of the ever-blessed
God.

Jesus is the only priest and a priest forever (Heb.
7:23-25). The author stresses the perpetuity of
Christ's priesthood proclaimed by the divine promise
(7:21). Whereas the levitical priests succeeded one
another in indefinite numbers, because their priesthood ceased at their death (7:23), Jesus, who is eternal, has no successors (7:24). The priests of the new
covenant, in fact, do not replace him but are his in-
struments, the ministers (Rom. 15:16) and ambassadors (2 Cor. 5:20) of Christ, the eternal priest.

From the perpetuity of the priesthood of our Savior
we must conclude (Heb. 7:25) that he is able to save
absolutely and definitively those who come to God
through his mediation. He is forever living and exer-
cising his priestly functions, offering to the heavenly
Father the humanity which he assumed and which,
immolated on the Cross, became the meritorious
cause of our salvation.

His priestly intercession did not cease with his
mortal life. His death was not for him, as for other
priests, the end of his priestly ministry. In him the
priesthood is not an accident that is separable from
his person. Mediator for our humanity (Rom. 8:34)
because he is the God-man, his function is perpetual,
since it is impossible that he could ever cease to be
what he is.

Christ's priesthood is everlasting (Heb. 7:24), permanent, unchangeable, inalienable, indefectible; infinite in duration and in power, it can never lose its efficacy. Hence he is able to save his own with a salvation that is perfect on every score (7:25). Better than Aaron (Ex. 28:29), our eternal priest has us always in his heart and is always available. And he is able to save to the furthest reaches of life and character, and finds no element intractable to his hand.

To intercede for us (7:25) is as close a description of Christ's priestly office as can be given in a few words. Christ's prayer is his supreme sacerdotal function. The specific nature, the efficacious exercise of his heavenly intercession may be indicated by Luke 22:32. Jesus is doing for his people now what he did for Peter in his hour of temptation — procuring for them the necessary spiritual strength to keep their faith from failing.

Intercession is most naturally understood as appeal to God for forgiveness and grace (Heb. 4:16). Our Lord's intercession actually includes every kind of mediation (9:24); all are included in it, and it cannot be limited by any or even all of them. His intercession is analogous to that of the Holy Spirit intervening before God in favor of the saints (Rom. 8:27).

The man-God in whom our humanity finds its reconciliation and reunion with God (Eph. 1:10) is himself a perpetual prayer by his very presence before God (Heb. 9:24). In him are expressed all our needs and aspirations, stamped with his unlimited power of intercession as the God-man. His intercession as our sponsor and our Paraclete (1 John 2:1) surrounds the throne of majesty like a cloud of fragrant incense. Yet the drawing near, the coming to God (Heb. 7:25) must be our act; our will and work are the conditions of his saving efficacy (4:16; 10:22).

The author concludes the parallel between the two priesthoods, that of the Levites and that of Christ, by affirming the holiness and absolute perfection of our Pontiff (7:26-28). These verses, which sum up and crown the preceding development, describe the personal traits of our high priest (7:26) and his priestly work (7:27), and establish a last contrast with the levitical priesthood in regard to appointment, nature, and consequent excellence (7:28). The conclusion is clear: Jesus is the ideal high priest, perfect in every respect in that office.

The qualities (7:26) of Christ the priest are first his holiness, which is expressed by three terms reflecting three aspects of holiness — in relation to God, to neighbor, and to oneself. Christ presents himself before God with an interior holiness of purity and sanctity which were the mature fruits of his dedication to God. In his relations with men he showed himself guileless, without malice or evil of any kind. Personally he was undefiled, without blemish of soul, free from any pollution such as would disqualify him for the office of priest or incapacitate him for the work of his office. The Aaronic priest was disqualified by a bodily blemish (Lev. 21:17-23); our priest is clean of heart as well.

Christ's personal perfection separates him completely from sinners; his moral transcendence corresponds to the transcendence of his nature. At the same time, he has the deepest compassion for sinners, and his perfect innocence before God enables him all the better to come to our assistance.

Finally, Christ's exaltation to the highest heavens shows the dignity of his person and the efficacy of his ministry. Such a high priest exalted to a position of highest dignity, pleading in the very presence of

God, is the high priest imperatively required by our need.

Christ's priestly excellence appears also in his priestly ministration (Heb. 7:27). Unlike the levitical priests, he has no personal sins to expiate, and his sacrifice is so efficacious that it needs no repetition. The absolute and definitive character of Christ's sacrifice is opposed to the sacrifices of the old law, which were indefinitely repeated, since they were impotent to assure salvation.

A general statement and final contrast (7:28) sum up the proof of the absolute superiority of Christ's priesthood. Each word is a contrast: on the one hand a simple fact, on the other an oath; formerly the law, now an institution which comes to replace the law; sinful priests, men encompassed with moral weakness, give way to the Saint *par excellence*; Aaron, a mere man, is replaced by our high priest, who is the very Son of God.

In loving adoration we admire Christ's wonderful priesthood. It is a filial (7:28) priesthood, heavenly (7:26) and eternal (7:24); a priesthood after the likeness of Melchizedek (7:15); a royal priesthood sanctioned by God's solemn oath (7:21); the priesthood of the new and superior covenant (7:22), of the better hope (7:19); the priesthood of the most holy Pontiff (7:26); a saving (7:25) priesthood, whose best expression is the prayer (7:25) of the priest who once and for all immolated himself as victim (7:27) for the sins of the world. Such is the everlasting priesthood of our Lord Jesus Christ, the perfect Son (7:28) and the high priest of the new covenant.

5.
Christic Our Mediator

HEBREWS 8:1-13

The main point in what we are saying is this: we have such a high priest, who has taken his seat at the right hand of the throne of the Majesty in heaven, ² minister of the sanctuary and of that true tabernacle set up, not by man, but by the Lord. ³ Now every high priest is appointed to offer gifts and sacrifices; hence the necessity for this one to have something to offer. ⁴ If he were on earth he would not be a priest, for there are priests already offering the gifts which the law prescribes. ⁵ They offer worship in a sanctuary which is only a copy and shadow of the heavenly one, for Moses, when about to erect the tabernacle, was warned, "See that you make everything according to the pattern shown you on the mountain." ⁶ Jesus has obtained a more excellent ministry now, just as he is mediator of a better covenant, founded on better promises.

⁷ If that first covenant had been faultless, there would have been no place for a second one. ⁸ But God, finding fault with them, says:

"Days are coming, says the Lord,
when I will make a new covenant
with the house of Israel
and with the house of Judah.
⁹ It will not be like the covenant I made
with their fathers
the day I took them by the hand
to lead them forth from the land of Egypt;
For they broke my covenant
and I grew weary of them, says the Lord.

¹⁰ But this is the covenant I will make with
   the house of Israel
  after those days, says the Lord:
  I will place my laws in their minds
   and I will write them upon their hearts;
  I will be their God
   and they shall be my people.
¹¹ And they shall not teach their fellow citizens
   or their brothers, saying, 'Know the Lord,'
   for all shall know me, from least to greatest.
¹² I will forgive their evildoing,
   and their sins I will remember no more."
¹³ When he says, "a new covenant," he declares the first
one obsolete. And what has become obsolete and has
grown old is close to disappearing.

Christ's priestly prayer (Heb. 7:25) as our mediator
before God's heavenly throne (8:1, 6) is a central
theme of the Epistle to the Hebrews. It finds its
earthly counterpart in our Lord's wonderful priestly
discourse to his disciples after the Last Supper (John
13–17).

Our Lord's presence in the heavenly sanctuary is a
perpetual reminder before God (Heb. 9:24) that his
sacrifice has been consummated and that our redemption has been effected. It is the pledge that our
salvation has been achieved in principle, and that all
that remains to be done is to apply its effects to those
who are not unworthy.

This heavenly presence of Jesus is already a prayer,
all the more so since it is the presence of a victim
(7:27) most agreeable to God, and the presence of a
Son (7:28) who has taken his seat in glory at the right

hand of his Father. His presence near God is evidently not a mere external formality, but a relation that is fully conscious and loving, and implies the closest possible intimacy between the divine Persons. These exchanges between the Son and his Father are the perpetual prayer of our resurrected Lord. By this prayer the Son expresses all his love to the Father and the Holy Spirit, and forever recommends us to God's merciful loving-kindness. That is how he is forever interceding for us (7:25).

Personally Christ is superior to the angels and to Moses (1:4—4:13), and his priesthood infinitely surpasses that of Aaron (4:14—7:28). Now the essential act of worship is sacrifice, and here again Christ's superiority appears. His sacrifice is infinitely superior to the ancient Mosaic sacrifices (8:1–10:18). The author argues from the superiority of the sanctuary in which Christ offers his sacrifice, and of the covenant which he establishes (8:1-13), and of his work of expiation (9:1-28) to conclude that Christ's unique and perfect sacrifice replaces all the sacrifices of the old law (10:1-18).

Christ's priestly work will stand in clearer light after an examination of the sanctuary in which it is performed (8:1-6) and of the conditions in which it is exercised (8:7-13). Two sanctuaries and two covenants are contrasted, with the new sanctuary and the new covenant replacing the old — a sanctuary of heaven and not of earth, a covenant of grace and not of works.

The eternal high priest has a work to do corresponding with his heavenly dignity (8:1-2). This work could not be fully accomplished on earth, which already had its limited system of service (8:3-4); this earthly liturgy, however, was only a shadow of the divine archetype which is realized in Christ (8:5-6).

Christ enthroned as high priest at God's right hand ministers, not in any earthly shrine, but in the heavenly sanctuary above, a tabernacle not made by human hands (8:1-2). The title "minister" indicates the reality of the sacerdotal functions he performs; his position at the right hand of God, sharing God's majesty, proclaims the omnipotence of his intercession.

Heaven is the true sanctuary, the true tabernacle of which the ancient sanctuary erected by Moses was the earthly copy (8:5), just as its ministry was a shadow of the heavenly offering (10:1). It is obvious that the copy must be inferior to the original, and Judaism is stamped with this second-hand character.

The fact and the scene of Christ's high priestly work are put in bold relief (8:3-4). A priest who ceased to do the work for which he had been appointed, namely to offer sacrifice, would no longer be a priest at all (8:3). Now Christ is a priest and so must have a sacrifice, one that is heavenly and everlasting. His sacrifice could not be merely terrestrial, since there were legally appointed priests here below (8:4). Now Christ was not of their race and, in any case, would not be doing more than they did.

As we have said, Christ ministers in the heavenly sanctuary, of which the earthly one was a mere copy or shadow (8:5). It can even be said that during his earthly life Jesus was not on earth (8:4); he lived here below and his priestly mediation began in this world, but it was entirely oriented toward heaven, transcending our earthly sphere.

In the revelation of the tabernacle to be built (Exod. 25:40), God was revealing at the same time the superior realities of which this first attempt at worship was the figurative and prophetic type. The tabernacle presented prefigures the ideas of the divine presence and of the realities of heaven — in short, of the messianic blessings that have their origin, their substance, and their consummation in heaven.

The conclusion (Heb. 8:6) of the preceding discussion declares that Christ's ministry is much superior to the liturgy of the temple; it also serves as a transition to the comparison of the two covenants (8:7-13). The value of a covenant is measured by the advantages it presents, and Christ has the very best to offer.

A covenant requires a mediator. Christ, truly and fully man (2:17) yet possessing the fullness of the divinity (Col. 2:9), is the only possible mediator between God and man (1 Tim. 2:5). He is the intermediary of grace (John 1:16-17) and of the definitive revelation (Heb. 1:1-2).

The levitical system was based on material promises relative to Israel's occupation of the land of Canaan (Deut. 29). The superior promises (Heb. 8:6) which our author has directly in mind are those which follow in the quotation from Jeremiah (8:8-12). They are better than those on which the old covenant was instituted, inasmuch as they promise forgiveness of sin (8:12), full and universal knowledge of God (8:11), and the writing of an inward law on the heart (8:10).

In Hebrews 7:21, the superiority of the Christian covenant was measured by that of the priesthood as determined by Psalm 109:4. Here the superiority of Christ's ministry is measured by that of the new covenant as determined by Jeremiah 31:31-34. The levitical system corresponded to a covenant which was recognized by the prophets as imperfect and transitory, for they spoke of the divine purpose to establish a new one that would be perfect and definitive. It follows that the new covenant, and the sacrifice on which it is founded, inherently surpass the old.

This section (Heb. 8:7-13) consists of a brief introduction (8:7-8a), the quotation from Jeremiah (8:8b-12), and a general conclusion (8:13).

First (8:7) we find again the same reasoning which was presented above for Christ's priesthood (7:11). God, who is infinitely wise, would not replace an institution by one less perfect or equal. If the first covenant had sufficed to bring men to perfection and salvation, or if its failure was due to some extrinsic, fortuitous cause, something independent of its specific nature, there would be no reason for change.

Actually the old covenant was not faultless, since it could not lead to true perfection (7:19). There was, then, a fault in the covenant itself, but the main fault lay with the Israelites in their failure to do their part (8:8). Hence we hear God's approach expressed by Jeremiah, in a passage which contains the prophet's most sublime teaching and is a landmark in Old Testament theology (Jer. 31:31-34).

After the catastrophe of the Exile, from which only a remnant will survive, a new and eternal covenant will be concluded (Heb. 8:8-9). This new covenant is characterized first of all by its interior quality (8:10). The law will no longer be a mere external charter but will become an inspiration which, under the influence of God's spirit, will give man a new heart (Ezek. 36:26-27). The new covenant will also be uniformly efficacious (Heb. 8:11) and will rest on God's complete forgiveness (8:12). All men will have immediate access to the divine presence, divine grace being the pledge of the covenant's efficacy.

The return from the Babylonian Exile was a figure of the great messianic deliverance; the new covenant

(8:8) replaces the old, which is set aside because of the people's failure to do their part despite God's kindness to them (8:9).

Instead of the old law written on tables of stone, there will be a new law engraved on the hearts of men (8:10). It will be interior and spiritual, becoming, so to speak, part of the believer's personality, since the heart, in Scripture, stands for a man's personal life, his moral character. God will put his law in the mind and engrave it on the heart, not only because it will be known and loved, but also because it will become an interior principle of light and action, identified with the soul, the interior principle of life. This transformation of the soul by grace will result in an intimate union of man with God. He will thus be their God whom alone they adore, love, and serve; and they will be his beloved people, showered with his gifts, divinized, and all this forever. It is by the Spirit of God that this promise is carried out (2 Cor. 3:3).

Another benefit of the new covenant is knowledge of God and of the things of God (Heb. 8:11). Many oracles announced the full and universal knowledge of the true religion as a blessing of messianic times (Is. 54:13; Joel 2:28-29). This again is a special function of God's holy and luminous Spirit (1 John 2:20, 27).

The last characteristic of the new alliance is that which contains the pledge of its efficacy, namely, the pardon of all sins (Heb. 8:12), an all-important theme in the author's view. The new covenant is founded on grace rather than on man's performance.

Our author's conclusion (8:13) goes beyond that which is established by the prophetic passage quoted. Jeremiah did not say clearly that the Mosaic law would be abrogated, and the Jews who heard him no doubt hoped that it would be renewed instead of replaced. We now know clearly God's plan.

The new covenant is not only better and founded on superior promises, but it supersedes the old, as was already suggested by its very name. The Messiah, the Cross of Jesus, the new covenant sound the death knell of the old law, which, however, receives in them its deepest fulfillment.

In a moment of silent recollection we adore once again our perfect mediator, who is always interceding for us before God's heavenly throne (7:25). How reassuring it is for us to know that at every moment our Savior prays for us and blesses our efforts from the heights of heaven!

In time of temptation and of distress, in our labors and sufferings, in the fulfillment of our humble daily tasks, even after our failures and cowardices, let us turn our eyes toward our Lord, through whom God blesses us with every spiritual blessing on high (Eph. 1:3). In fact, we have already been introduced there in a mysterious way in Christ (Eph. 2:6), who has entered as our forerunner (Heb. 6:20) and has prepared a place for us (John 14:2-3).

6.

The Excellence of Christ's Sacrifice

HEBREWS 9:1-12

The first covenant had regulations for worship and an earthly sanctuary. ² For a tabernacle was constructed, the outer one, in which were the lampstand, the table, and the showbread; this was called the holy place. ³ Behind the second veil was the tabernacle called the holy of holies, ⁴ in which were the golden altar of incense and the ark of the covenant entirely covered with gold. In the ark were the golden jar containing the manna, the rod of Aaron which had blossomed, and the tablets of the covenant. ⁵ Above the ark were the cherubim of glory overshadowing the place of expiation. We cannot speak now of each of these in detail. ⁶ These were the arrangements for worship. In performing their service the priests used to go into the outer tabernacle constantly, ⁷ but only the high priest went into the inner one, and that but once a year, with the blood which he offered for himself and for the sins of the people. ⁸ The Holy Spirit was showing thereby that while the first tabernacle was still standing, the way into the sanctuary had not yet been revealed. ⁹ This is a symbol of the present time, in which gifts and sacrifices are offered that can never make perfect the conscience of the worshiper, ¹⁰ but can only cleanse in matters of food and drink and various ritual washings: regulations concerning the flesh, imposed until the time of the new order.

¹¹ But when Christ came as high priest of the good things which have come to be, he entered once for all into the

sanctuary, passing through the greater and more perfect tabernacle not made by hands, that is, not belonging to this creation. [12] He entered, not with the blood of goats and calves, but with his own blood, and achieved eternal redemption.

The triumphant refrain, "We have a priest" (Heb. 4:14, 15; 8:1; 10:21), expresses succinctly the major theme of the Epistle to the Hebrews — the absolute superiority of Christ's priesthood. The basic reason for the excellence of his priesthood (4:14–7:28) is the supereminence of Christ's sacrifice (8:1–10:18).

The scene and the new conditions of Christ's priestly work have been examined: Jesus is the minister of the heavenly sanctuary and the mediator of a new covenant (ch. 8). The writer now goes on to consider in detail the essential act by which Christ has inaugurated this sanctuary and sealed the new covenant, namely, his sacrifice, comparing it with the priestly service of the levitical system (ch. 9).

For point of comparison, the sacred writer takes the most august forms of both systems: the service of the Day of Atonement (Yom Kippur), and the Passion and Ascension of our Lord. The author sees in the feast of Atonement a type or foreshadowing of Christ's sacrifice of expiation. Like the levitical high priest, Jesus brings into the holy of holies (heaven) the blood of the victim immolated in the holy or outer sanctuary (Calvary).

The author describes first the old sanctuary and the rites of expiation, insisting on their figurative character (9:1-10). The atonement of Christ was symbolized by these ancient rites. The blood of Christ is at the same time expiation, testament, and covenant (9:11-22), and it opens heaven (9:23-28).

The sacred writer depicts with affectionate reverence the ordered arrangements of the old sanctuary and its furniture, and the limited privileges of the old priesthood (9:1-10). He recalls the material furnishings of the tabernacle (9:1-5) in order to characterize better the legal worship and, in particular, the rite of expiation, which was the highlight of the ceremonial system (9:6-10).

A knowledge of the chief points in the ceremonial of the Day of Atonement (Lev. 16) is necessary for the understanding of this chapter. The high priest killed a bullock as a sin-offering for himself and his house (the priesthood), and taking the blood, entered the innermost shrine, the holy of holies, where he sprinkled the blood upon the mercy seat. On this day alone was entrance allowed to the holy of holies, the shrine of the manifested Presence of God (Exod. 25:22). Having cleansed, consecrated, and made atonement for the priesthood by the sprinkling, the high priest came back, killed a goat as a sin offering for the people, and sprinkled its blood in the same manner. The golden altar of incense in the holy place and the altar of burnt offering in the outer court were also cleansed by the blood of both victims.

The temple described (Heb. 9:1-5) is not Herod's but the original Mosaic tabernacle. Herod's monument, notwithstanding its splendor, no longer sheltered the ark of the covenant, symbol of God's presence among his people. In Herod's temple the annual sprinkling of the blood was performed on the spot where the mercy seat would have stood.

The author has genuine admiration and reverence for the beauty and majesty of the Mosaic worship and for the sacred treasures of the past, especially since they will help to understand the gospel better.

The sanctuary is described first (9:2-5) and then its ritual (9:6-10). The adjective "earthly" (9:1) already introduces the essentially transitory and inferior nature of this sanctuary and its liturgy, as opposed to the sanctuary which is not of this world (8:2) and Christ's superior ministry (8:6).

Twelve loaves of bread on the golden table (9:2) represented the people's grateful acknowledgment that they owed everything to their God. A first curtain led from the outer court into the holy place (9:3). The golden altar of incense stood in the holy place (Exod. 30:6), not in the holy of holies as the text suggests (9:4). This unimportant misstatement is probably due to the fact that the author is describing what he knew only from the Septuagint, which is ambiguous. His vague association of the ark with the altar of incense stresses the liturgical and symbolic relation between these two objects. They typified the two innermost conceptions of the heavenly sanctuary — the manifestations of God and Christ's intercession for us.

According to 1 Kings 8:9 and 2 Chronicles 5:10, there was nothing in the ark except the tablets of the covenant. Moses gave orders to put the golden urn (Exod. 16:34) and the rod of Aaron (Num. 17:25) in the tabernacle near the ark. Here our author does not pay too much attention to these details (Heb. 9:4), which are immaterial to his viewpoint. He simply groups together all the best souvenirs of God's merciful intervention in favor of his chosen people.

The mercy seat (9:5) above the ark was so called because on it, by the sprinkling of the blood, expiation was made for the sins of the people on the Day of

Atonement (Lev. 16:14-16). The cherubim are ''of glory'' (9:5) because with the propitiatory their wings formed the throne of God's glory and majesty (Exod. 15:22), the visible pedestal for the invisible presence.

The details of the levitical worship (Heb. 9:6-10) follow the description of the sanctuary. The priests discharged their sacred duties daily in the outer shrine, particularly the burning of incense on the small altar; but the inner shrine was entered only once a year, on the Day of Atonement, when the high priest, passing through the curtain which normally barred access to the divine presence, presented the sacrificial blood as a propitiation for his own sins and those of the people.

Verses 8-10 explain the symbolism of these prescriptions relative to the tabernacle and its arrangements. The Holy Spirit, author of Scriptures, indicated by this ceremonial that the way leading to the true holy place, the heavenly sanctuary, was not yet opened, as long as the levitical worship was not replaced (9:8).

Under the ancient law the people had no direct access to God. Christ is now the unobstructed way to God for all believers (John 14:6; Heb. 10:19). Access to God is the final end and object of the priesthood and is fully realized in Christ alone.

The levitical sacrifices could not produce the inward purity (9:9) which is now available in messianic times. These are times of true reformation (9:10), of setting aright, of rectifying the false relation in which fallen men stood with God.

The ''first tabernacle'' here (9:8-9) does not refer to place, as in verse 2, but to time, and is contrasted with the more perfect tabernacle of the good things to come (9:11). The ''present time'' (9:9) is the old economy. Assertions like this (9:8) give sanction to the Church's system of typical interpretation of the Old Testament.

Our Lord's priestly work, his sacrifice, is the archetype of the ritual for the feast of Atonement (9:11-28). On it rests the new covenant, whose fruition is yet to be revealed in glory. Two main points come into consideration: the entrance of the high priest into the divine presence, and the fact that the entrance was made with blood. Christ's saving work is first described generally (9:11-12), and then the truths suggested by the shedding of his blood (9:13-22) and by his entrance into the heavenly sanctuary (9:23-28) are presented in detail.

The work of Christ as high priest of the new order stands in sovereign superiority over the ancient order in regard to scene and offering and efficacy. The tabernacle in which he ministered was not of this creation but heavenly (9:11b). The blood through which he entered before God was not that of sacrificed animals but his own (9:12a). The redemption which he obtained was not for a brief time but for ever (9:12b).

Christ is mediator of spiritual and eternal blessings: forgiveness, sanctification, eternal life, eternal redemption (9:12), and eternal inheritance (9:15). These "good things" are still to come (9:11), since men have yet to enter into the full possession of their inheritance.

Heaven is considered as a temple which Jesus enters by his Ascension, to arrive at the holy of holies, God's presence, where every imperfection disappears. As the Jewish high priest passed through the different parts of the tabernacle on the Day of Atonement, so also Christ, after his resurrection, enters the ideal sanctuary of heaven. And while the Jewish priest entered into the inner shrine with the blood of animals,

Christ entered the heavenly shrine with his own blood (9:12a). Finally, the Jewish priest entered year by year; Christ entered once for all.

The offering of Christ's blood is incomparably superior to sacrifices of the blood of goats and calves (9:13-14) because it is the life (Lev. 17:11) of a Person, the Christ, not of irrational beasts (Heb. 10:4). Then, too, Christ was both priest and sacrificial victim (9:12), and his offering was made once for all (9:12, 25-26; 10:11-12) in the heavenly tabernacle (9:24). It was a voluntary act (10:9; cf. John 10:17-18), accomplished through the "eternal spirit" (9:14), and consequently the efficacy of his sacrifice remains for all time (10:14). Its force is final and definitive, its character absolute; its value is eternal, owing to his personality, the eternal spirit of his divinity (9:14).

Many of these thoughts are developed in Hebrews (9:13-28); we are reserving them for further consideration. Special notice, however, should be given at this point to the fact that Christ's offering of himself to his Father is not merely his self-oblation on Calvary; it includes also the subsequent presentation of himself as victim in heaven. His sacrifice was not fully completed until after his resurrection from the dead and his appearance before the Father in the innermost sanctuary of heaven, bringing with him the merits of his Cross and Passion.

This entry of Jesus into heaven, once and for all, is one of the major themes of the Epistle to the Hebrews. Christ's priesthood, which was imparted to him at the Incarnation (*sacrificium nativum*) was ratified (*ratum*) by this solemn entry and return to the Father.

7.

The Blood of Christ - A Perfect Sacrifice

HEBREWS 9:13-28

For if the blood of goats and bulls and the sprinkling of a heifer's ashes can sanctify those who are defiled so that their flesh is cleansed, [14] how much more will the blood of Christ, who through the eternal spirit offered himself up unblemished to God, cleanse our consciences from dead works to worship the living God!

[15] This is why he is mediator of a new covenant: since his death has taken place for deliverance from transgressions committed under the first covenant, those who are called may receive the promised eternal inheritance. [16] Where there is a testament, it is necessary that the death of the testator be confirmed. [17] For a testament comes into force only in the case of death; it has no force while the testator is alive. [18] Hence, not even the first covenant was inaugurated without blood. [19] When Moses had read all the commandments of the law of the people, he took the blood of goats and calves, together with water and crimson wool and hyssop, and sprinkled the book and all the people, [20] saying, "This is the blood of the covenant which God has enjoined upon you." [21] He also sprinkled the tabernacle and all the vessels of worship with blood. [22] According to the law almost everything is purified by blood, and without the shedding of blood there is no forgiveness.

[23] It was necessary that the copies of the heavenly models be purified in this way, but the heavenly realities themselves called for better sacrifices. [24] For Christ did not

enter into a sanctuary made by hands, a mere copy of the true one; he entered heaven itself that he might appear before God now on our behalf. [25] Not that he might offer himself there again and again, as the high priest enters year after year into the sanctuary with blood that is not his own; [26] if that were so, he would have had to suffer death over and over from the creation of the world. But now he has appeared at the end of the ages to take away sins once for all by his sacrifice. [27] Just as it is appointed that men die once, and after death be judged, [28] so Christ was offered up once to take away the sins of many; he will appear a second time not to take away sin but to bring salvation to those who eagerly await him.

Christ's priesthood is a wonderful mystery whose unfathomable depths reach infinitely beyond the possibilities of our essentially limited human intelligence. Its superiority and uniqueness (Heb. 4:14–7:28) is based ultimately on the excellence of his sacrifice (8:1–10:18).

After a summary exposition (9:11-12), the sacred writer explains in detail the value and efficacy of Christ's sacrifice. He shows the exceptional power of the blood of Christ as a means of expiation, a purifying power, by contrast with the expiatory victims of the Old Testament (9:13-15); then as a testament, a characteristic proper to his sacrifice (9:16-17); finally as the ratification of the new covenant, of which the alliance on Mount Sinai was but a feeble figure (9:18-22).

The Old Testament ritual had a limited validity in procuring the legal, ceremonial purity which enabled the Jew to enjoy the full privileges of his covenant worship and fellowship with God's people. Two typical examples of the purificatory levitical sacrifices are (9:13) the yearly sacrifices of goats and bulls on the Day of Atonement (Lev. 16), and the occasional sacrifice of a red heifer (Num. 19).

In contrast with the Old Testament sacrifices, the superiority of Christ's sacrifice appears in every respect. The blood of Christ (Heb. 9:14) means his life given up for the sake of men. Christ offers himself by his eternal spirit, his divine nature, which, because of its omnipotence and eternity, communicates to the shedding of his blood an infinite value and eternal efficacy. Christ's sacrifice is thus lifted from its local environment into the region of eternity by its animating spirit — a wonderful paradox of death producing eternal life.

The passivity of the animals is also contrasted with Christ's voluntary offering: he offers himself and is, as Saint Epiphanius puts it, "at the same time temple and victim, priest and altar, God and man, king and high priest."

The Old Testament victim was to be without blemish (Exod. 29:1, 38). That which was required outwardly for the levitical victims is satisfied absolutely by Christ's moral perfection, his boundless holiness (1 Peter 1:19), his stainless personality, his sinless nature. Hence the difference in the effects produced. Instead of a mere cleansing of the flesh (an external purity), the dead works of sin (9:14) are pardoned. Note how the effects of sin are corruption and death, alienation from God; in Christ, man's conscience is now free, pure, and at peace with God.

This purity is not an end but the means of a new life of service and worship worthy of him who alone truly lives and gives life. To serve and adore the living God is the purpose of all human existence, of all religion and divine revelation, and the aim and object of all priestly ministry.

Christ's expiation inaugurates a new covenant (9:15). His death expiates the sins against which the old covenant was helpless; the divine promises are now fulfilled, a new era begins. Christ's death was necessary because of his function as priestly mediator. Priesthood and covenant are intimately related. Now a covenant (9:15) requires the shedding of blood (Exod. 24:6-8), and the death of the testator gives right to the inheritance (Heb. 9:16-17). There is a play on the Greek word which means both "alliance" (9:15, 18-20) and "testament" (9:16-17). The testament idea is a Jewish refinement suggested by the mention of inheritance (9:15).

The death of Christ was not a sign of weakness but rather an essential condition of the establishment of the messianic kingdom and of the inheritance of those messianic blessings of which Christ was the primary heir and sole dispenser.

The blood of Christ inaugurated the new covenant (9:18-22). These verses have been styled the mysticism of blood, its spiritual theology. There were three principal uses of blood in the Old Testament: for the covenant sacrifice (9:18-21), for purification, and for expiation. All this drama of blood announced the necessity of convenience of our Lord's bloody death, which is clearly superior to the covenant it replaces.

The dedication of the first covenant is described in Exodus 24:1-8. Our writer clearly regards the Day of Atonement as an annual renewal of this dedication ceremony. Hence the freedom with which he alters the narrative of Exodus (Heb. 10:18-21).

Christ's blood was the means by which the new covenant was inaugurated (1 Cor. 11:25); it introduced and confirmed God's people in the covenant fellowship with God (Heb. 4:16; 7:25). In fact, the shedding of Christ's redemptive blood is the only objective source of salvation (1 Cor. 1:30). The blood of Christ is the perfect sacrifice which opens the perfect sanctuary of heaven and needs no repetition because of its absolute perfection (9:23-28). These verses draw a parallel between the acts of the Jewish high priest on the Day of Atonement and their fulfillment by our Lord in the heavenly sanctuary.

The sacrifices purifying the earthly sanctuary prefigured the more perfect sacrifice of Christ, which purifies for heaven (9:23). It is a perfect sacrifice because it opens heaven itself (9:24), has no need of repetition (9:25-26a), and vanquishes sin forever (9:26b). It thus guarantees for the faithful the salvation which Christ will consummate in glory at the time of his second coming, the glorious Parousia (9:27-28).

The purification required for both the earthly and the heavenly sanctuaries (9:23) does not necessarily presuppose defilement. It is a rite of consecration and dedication. The living Christ fulfills in heaven what was represented by the blood of victims upon earth.

The superiority of the heavenly sanctuary appears in three respects (9:24), viz., it is not man-made but God's masterpiece; it is the model and reality imitated imperfectly by the earthly sanctuary; and God, who remained invisible to the high priest, is completely accessible to its minister, Christ.

Like Aaron (Exod. 28:29), who presented himself before the ark of the covenant on behalf of his people, Christ enters heaven to take care of our interests and to make ready for our reception. Christ's priesthood is eternal (Heb. 7:23-24), and it is as Savior and Pontiff that he is always living to plead on our behalf (7:25). This priestly intercession is Christ's ministry in the heavenly sanctuary (8:1-2), renewing and continuing the unique sacrifice of the Cross. It is a description in ritual, liturgical language of Christ's enthronement at the right hand of glory, in the plenitude of divine splendor and the exercise of divine omnipotence (1:3; 2:5-9; 10:12). All power is now his in recognition of his sacrifice, his redemptive work here below. This is the supreme, essential exercise of his priestly ministry.

In contrast with the sacrifices of the old covenant, which, because of their imperfection, were repeated indefinitely (9:25), Christ's sacrificial death is absolute and decisive in its efficacy. It was quite natural and normal that Christ, like other men, should only die once (9:26-27), yet his death occupies the center of the history of salvation and inaugurates the eschatological era, the final and definitive age in the successive periods of history. The second coming, the glorious Parousia, is the last day (1 Cor. 1:8).

The first coming of Christ placed him in direct relation with sin (Rom. 8:3; 2 Cor. 5:21). Redemption having been accomplished, the new and final manifestation of the Savior will be not as victim but as conqueror (9:28). Christians await this glorious return, which will include the last judgment (Rom. 2:6), with complete and permanent salvation for the elect. As the Israelites on the Day of Atonement eagerly awaited the reappearance of their high priest after he had entered into the holy of holies, so the Christian people wait for Christ's Parousia, knowing that he will then dispense to his people the final and eternal benefits of his one sacrifice.

8.

The Perfect Efficacy of Christ's Sacrifice

HEBREWS 10:1-18

Since the law had only a shadow of the good things to come, and no real image of them, it was never able to perfect the worshipers by the same sacrifices offered continually year after year. ² Were matters otherwise, the priests would have stopped offering them, for the worshipers, once cleansed, would have had no sin on their conscience. ³ But through those sacrifices there came only a yearly recalling of sins, ⁴ because it is impossible for the blood of bulls and goats to take sins away. ⁵ Wherefore, on coming into the world, Jesus said:

"Sacrifice and offering you did not desire,
but a body you have prepared for me;
⁶ Holocausts and sin offerings you took no delight in.
⁷ Then I said, 'As is written of me in the book,
I have come to do your will, O God.' "
⁸ First he says,
"Sacrifices and offerings, holocausts and sin offerings,
you neither desired nor delighted in."
(These are offered according to the prescriptions of the law.) ⁹ Then he says,
"I have come to do your will."
In other words, he takes away the first covenant to establish the second.
¹⁰ By this "will," we have been sanctified through the offering of the body of Jesus Christ once for all. ¹¹ Every other priest stands ministering day by day, and offering again

65

and again those same sacrifices which can never take away sins. [12] But Jesus offered one sacrifice for sins and took his seat forever at the right hand of God; [13] now he waits until his enemies are placed beneath his feet. [14] By one offering he has forever perfected those who are being sanctified. [15] The Holy Spirit attests this to us, for after saying,

[16] "This is the covenant I will make with them
    after those days, says the Lord:
  I will put my laws in their hearts
    and I will write them on their minds,"
[17] he also says,
    "Their sins and their transgressions
      I will remember no more."
[18] Once these have been forgiven, there is no further offering for sin.

Christ is the only priest, the *catholic* (universal) priest, according to Tertullian's splendid expression, *Christus Iesus Catholicus Patris Sacerdos* (PL, 2, 405). His sacrifice, in fact, is unique and perfect, replacing all the ancient sacrifices (Heb. 10:1-18).

In the preceding section (9:1-28), the excellence of Christ's priestly work was shown by comparison with the service of the old covenant on the Day of Atonement. Christ offered himself once for all, and coming forth in due time from the divine presence, he will proclaim the consummation of his work. This comparison is now extended from the general representative sacrifice to the levitical sacrifices generally.

The author shows that the repetition of these sacrifices is a sign of their inherent weakness and provisional office (10:1-4). In contrast with them, he describes the true nature of Christ's sacrifice (10:5-10).

He then shows its eternal and infinite efficacy because of Christ's present position of kingly majesty (10:11-14), and the consequent fulfillment in him of the oracles of the Old Testament prophets relative to the new covenant (10:15-18).

The sacrifices of the Mosaic system could not bring perfection, for what they did had to be reiterated (10:1); and such repetition would not have been required if they had been spiritually efficacious (10:2), producing a true and final atonement. Viewed in their real character, they were designed to declare a need which they did not satisfy (10:3) and which essentially they could not satisfy (10:4).

The ancient law, an insubstantial shadow, a more or less distorted outline without detail, is contrasted with the perfect reality of the messianic blessings of grace and glory. The old law witnessed to grace and truth beyond and outside itself; the new law is the pledge and means through which our fellowship with God is realized in Christ. Unlike the new, the old law could not give interior perfection or effect pardon of sin. Perfection here (10:1), as in verse 14, is purification of conscience, the pardon of sins, and the consequent union with God in a plenitude of grace.

Christ's sacrifice, as Chrysostom puts it, is a perfect remedy which effects a perfect cure and needs no repetition. Unlike the Old Testament sacrifice, it is a display of strength and not a mere confession of weakness. It brings about a lasting and adequate relationship with God.

The levitical sacrifices, however, had an important function to fulfill in the discipline of men. Their repetition, which showed their inefficacy, kept alive the senses (remembrance) of sin. The use of the word *remembrance* suggests a contrast between the Jewish sacrifices and the Christian Eucharist. In the ancient sacrifices there was a remembrance of sin. They were instituted to keep fresh the thought of responsibility for sin, against which they were powerless. Christ instituted the Eucharist in remembrance of himself, to bring to men's minds the recollection of the eternal salvation which he has accomplished.

Hence also the necessary repetition of the Eucharistic sacrifice, which is the sign and symbol of the sacrifice of the Cross and of the liturgy of heaven. It is one with that of the Cross and applies to the faithful the infinite merits of the unique sacrifice of Calvary, but in a limited way according to our dispositions.

The spiritual inefficacy of the levitical sacrifices indicated by their repetition (10:2) is evident also from their very nature (10:4). The physical suffering and death of an irrational creature, unwilling and unconscious, can make no atonement for man's sin; such a sacrifice cannot be more than a symbol, a sign (9:13). It establishes no real community between the offerer and the victim.

We thus see again the reason why the writer of Hebrews puts such stress on the Incarnation and the real human experience of Christ. Jesus becomes man not merely that he may sympathize with us, but that he may offer himself for us. Vicarious sacrifice is a principle profoundly true and valid, but he who sacrifices himself for others must first be one with them. He must also be one with God (10:5-18), to whom the sacrifice is directed; and this is the heart of the matter of Christ's priestly mediation, his eternal priesthood. Christ's sacrifice is the one valid sacrifice perfectly fulfilling God's will (10:5-10). This truth is expressed in the language of the Psalmist (Ps. 40:7-9). The quote (Heb. 10:5-7) includes interesting but unimportant variants from the original.

Christ, coming into the world, recognizes that his obedience is the only sacrifice agreeable to God (10:5-6), and so in full submission offers himself to his Father (10:7). In so doing he abolished the ancient levitical sacrifices (10:8-9) and became forever the cause and source of our sanctification (10:10).

In the original poem (Ps. 40), the Psalmist remembers the help he has received from God (vv.2-4) and acknowledges God's great and wonderful goodness (vv.5-6). He concludes that the best way to thank God is to obey his precepts (vv.7-9) and publish far and wide his wondrous works (vv.10-11). The psalm affirms the common prophetic doctrine that sacrifice is in itself of no value apart from the dispositions of heart which it is intended to represent (Amos 5:21-24). Our quote implies the absolute rejection of all the ancient legal sacrifices.

Prompt and absolute obedience will be the law of our Lord's life, and his voluntary immolation its climax. The body of the incarnate Son was prepared for him by God that it might be the organ of his perfect obedience in life and particularly in death.

The oracles of the prophets, the Old Testament figures, persons and facts, the symbol of the legal ceremonies, the moral and sapiential precepts describing the ideal just man, all the inspired books of the Old Testament (10:7) revealed God's plan for his own glory and the salvation of men. All that God expected of him Christ accepted in perfect obedience, and by his immolation on Calvary established the new covenant and sanctified us in this will (10:9-10). We are saved, in fact, by our total acceptance of God's will, by Christ's union with the will of God, and by our union through Christ in that same divine will, which is grounded on infinite wisdom and expressed in saving love. "In his will is our peace."

A view of the efficacy of Christ's priestly work (10:11-14) follows the description of its historical realization as a fulfillment of the revealed will of God (10:5-10). Whereas the levitical priest repeated his ineffective ministry each day (10:11), Jesus, by his one sacrifice, expiated forever all sins, glorified his Father, obtained for us pardon, holiness, and salvation, and merited for himself full triumph (10:12). Seated in heaven at the right hand of God, he waits until his enemies are reduced to complete subjection, this final and definitive victory being now just a matter of time (10:13-14).

Another feature of Christ's priestly work which marks its infinite superiority is the fact that his sacrifice is not only pleasing to God but has an absolute power, issuing from Christ's perfect sovereignty. This glorification of Christ, his enthronement at God's right hand, is a token of his having thoroughly accomplished his work, and a sign of the efficacy and perfection of his redemptive mission here on earth. Christ's sanctifying work is complete and definitive, yet man's attainment of purification in Christ is gradual and progressive (10:14).

The warlike metaphor in 10:13 is a reprise of Psalm 109:1 and a negative presentation of redemption as a conflict between good and evil, culminating ultimately in a victory over the devil (Heb. 2:14) and all the powers of wickedness throughout the ages.

The author goes back in conclusion to the testimony of the prophet Jeremiah (Jer. 31:33-34), showing in Christ the fulfillment of the prophetic description of the new covenant (Heb. 10:15-18). A characteristic of that covenant announced by the prophet and realized by Christ is the full and final forgiveness of all sins. It follows that there is no more place in the new economy for the levitical sacrifices, which were in any case inoperative.

Whether we regard Christ in his own nature or in his priesthood and the benefits thereby accruing to mankind, the result is uniformly the same — namely, that he has an absolute claim to exclusive obedience. He supersedes all that went before him; he deserves undivided allegiance, and the Mosaic system is now completely antiquated.

Spiritual purification (10:2, 10, 14), pardon of sin and salvation (10:4, 6, 11, 12, 17, 18), and union with God (10:1, 14) — these are the fruits of Christ's sacrifice. Christ alone makes us perfect adorers of God, giving us the inward purity which permits access to God's presence. That is his priestly office and the ultimate proof of the superiority and uniqueness of his sacrifice and priesthood.

POPULAR LITURGICAL LIBRARY

CHRIST'S PRIESTHOOD ACCORDING TO THE EPISTLE TO THE HEBREWS is but one item in the *Popular Liturgical Library,* a series of books, pamphlets, leaflets, prints, periodicals on the

EUCHARISTIC LITURGY	**FAMILY LIFE**
SACRAMENTS	**SACRED SCRIPTURE**
DIVINE OFFICE	**LITURGICAL YEAR**
SACRED SONG	**CATECHETICS**

A complete, free, descriptive catalog will be sent gladly upon request. Address:

THE LITURGICAL PRESS,
Collegeville, Minnesota 56321